60 000 023 352

KT-489-318

Snappy Sharks

by Ruth Owen

Editorial consultant: Mitch Cronick

ticktock

Northamptonshire Libraries & Information Service	
60 000 023 352	
Peters	03-Nov-2009
C597.3	£3.99

CONTENTS

Words in **bold** are explained in the glossary.

We love sharks!

Sharks live in the sea.

4

Some sharks have big teeth.

Great white shark

This shark **hunts** for **seals**, fish and little sharks!

Fin

7

Snappy shark teeth

This great white shark's tooth
is six centimetres long!

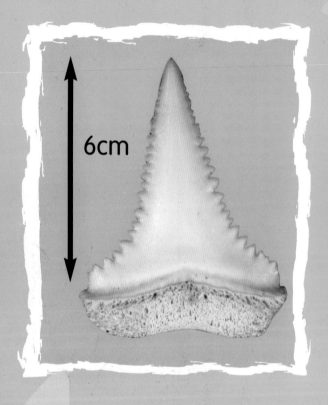

6cm

8

Teeth

Hammerhead shark

This shark's big eyes
help it to see food.

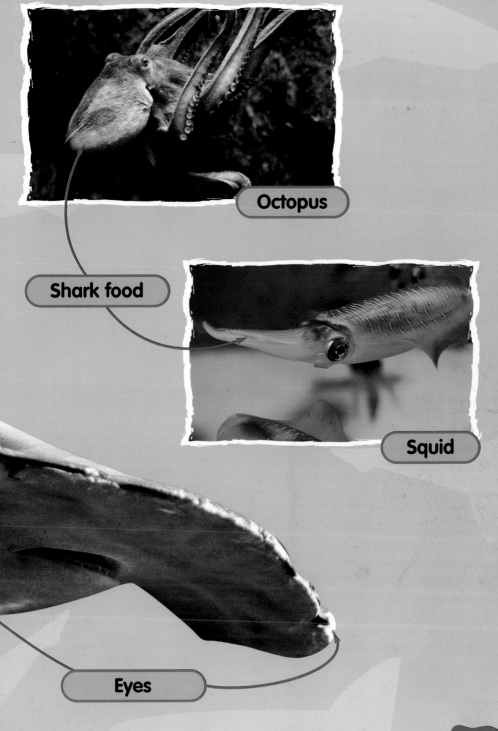

Octopus

Shark food

Squid

Eyes

11

Super shark noses

A shark has a good **sense** of smell. It can smell a fish 500 metres away!

13

The biggest shark!

A whale shark is very big.
It's as long as 20 children.

15

Tiger shark

Young tiger sharks have **stripes**.

Shark eggs

Some shark mums lay eggs.

Eggs

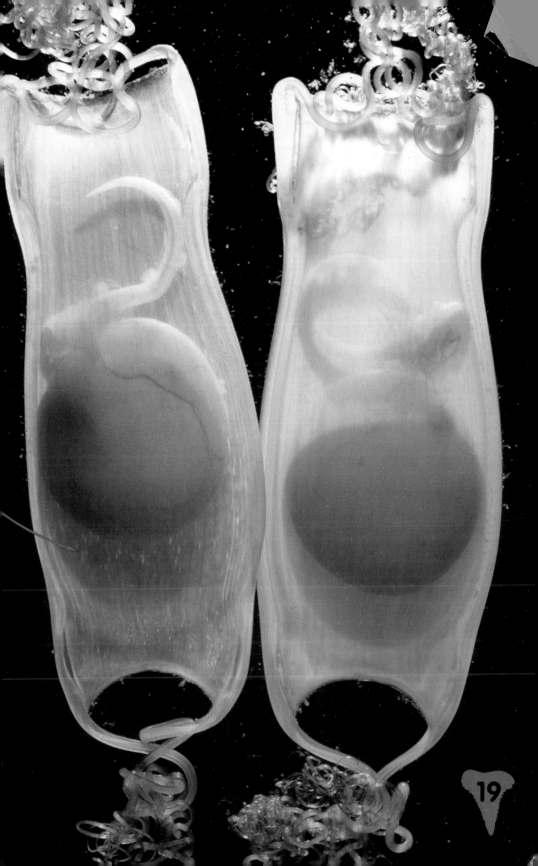

Shark babies

Some shark mums give birth to live babies, not eggs.

The little babies swim off to hunt.

Glossary

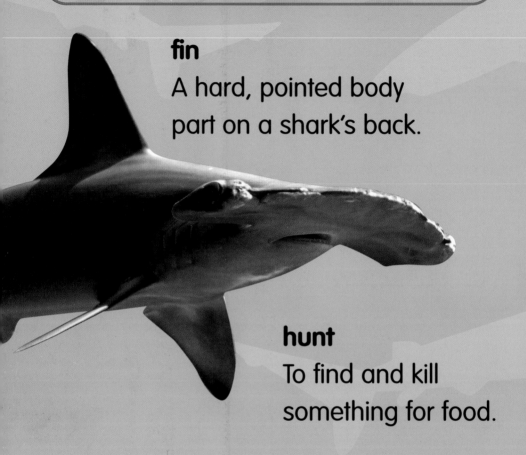

fin

A hard, pointed body part on a shark's back.

hunt

To find and kill something for food.

seal

A sea animal with a fat, smooth body.

sense
Seeing, hearing, smelling, touching and tasting are all senses.

stripes
Long, thin patterns of different colours.

Index

Publisher: Melissa Fairley
Studio Manager: Sara Greasley
Editor: Emma Dods
Designer: Trudi Webb
Production Controller: Ed Green
Production Manager: Suzy Kelly

ISBN: 978 1 84898 115 7

Copyright © ticktock Entertainment Ltd 2009
First published in Great Britain in 2009 by ticktock Media Ltd.,
The Old Sawmill, 103 Goods Station Road, Tunbridge Wells, Kent TN1 2DP

Printed in China
9 8 7 6 5 4 3 2 1

A CIP catalogue record for this book is available from the British Library. All rights reserved. No part of this publication may be reproduced, copied, stored in a retrieval system or transmitted in any form or by any means electronic, mechanical, photocopying, recording or otherwise without prior written permission of the copyright owner.

Picture credits (t=top, b=bottom, c=centre, l=left, r=right, OFC= outside front cover, OBC=outside back cover):
age footstock/SuperStock: 16–17, 23b. iStock: 14–15. Shutterstock: OFC, 1, 2, 4, 8, 10–11 all, 12–13, 16–17 background, 18, 22t, 22b, 23t, OBC. Mauritius/SuperStock: 9. Mike Parry/Minden Pictures/FLPA: 5, 6–7.
© Doug Perrine/SeaPics.com: 20–21. D P Wilson/FLPA: 19.

Every effort has been made to trace the copyright holders, and we apologize in advance for any unintentional omissions. We would be pleased to insert the appropriate acknowledgements in any subsequent edition of this publication.